LUNCHBOX
EXPRESS

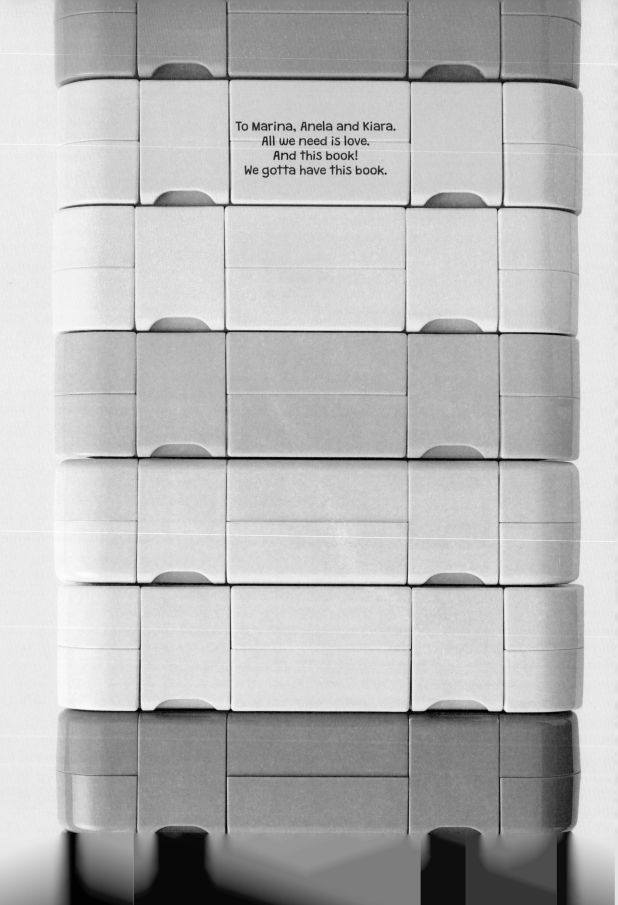

To Marina, Anela and Kiara.
All we need is love.
And this book!
We gotta have this book.

George Georgievski

Australia's School Lunchbox Dad

 plum. Pan Macmillan Australia

CONTENTS

INTRODUCTION

I was fortunate to have been born into a family that really values togetherness, fun and, above all, love. When I was a child, my father knew how to get the best out of me, always having high expectations, but never ruling with an iron fist. He led with love and encouraged me to forge my own path in life, to make good choices and become a critical thinker.

My dad taught me lessons in unconventional ways – a little like Mr Miyagi from *The Karate Kid* (wax on, wax off) – such as our extremely long chess games. At his insistence we would play only one move per day, each move carefully considered, so a game could go on for six months! Just before he died, he asked me if I remembered our chess games and I confessed that I had actually found them a bit boring. He revealed that the point had never been chess. Our slow games had been his way of teaching me the art of patience, perseverance and, most importantly, what he saw as the role of the king – to protect and make way for the queen. For my dad, that queen was my mum, who has always been the glue holding our family together. I've taken this lesson into my life, and my queens (my mum, sister, wife and daughters) are everything to me. They are my reason for being and I see my job as to stand behind them, supporting them in whatever way I can.

People often ask me about my tattoos. One shows two chess pieces: a king in front of a pawn. This reminds me to always follow in my father's footsteps. The other is a portrait of my parents when they were young. This is a reminder to live my life with love as my guide.

My wife, Marina, used to look after the morning routine for our family because I started work early. But one day, I was off work sick and happened to catch the morning commotion of getting the girls ready and their lunches organised. Marina, who was running around trying to get everything done, told me that this was what it was like every day! It just didn't feel right that my wife, the woman I love so much, was having to start her day in such a stressful way. So, I started making the lunches. It was one thing I could do to instantly take some of the load off Marina. To start with, I had NO idea what to pack in the girls' lunchboxes, so I started looking for ideas online. Everything was either too complicated to do quickly in the morning or too confusing. I just wanted something simple, so I gave up looking online and decided I would do my own thing. We lead a healthy lifestyle, and I felt confident I could pack nutritionally balanced lunchboxes filled with things my girls would actually eat. And that's how this all started.

One day, the girls brought home a note from their teacher complimenting my lunches and suggesting I post my lunchbox ideas on social media. My Instagram page (@schoollunchbox) was born, and the rest is history. Since then, I've made it my mission to create healthy, fun, varied and FAST (five minutes to throw together, honestly!) lunches for my girls, and to inspire other parents to do the same. As well as presenting fruit and veggies in interesting ways, I started coming up with recipes of my own, creating new takes on old lunchbox favourites and making fast and simple creations using everyday foods. I now have more than 100,000 followers from all over the world, I am an ambassador for the lunchbox company Stuck On You and I travel around the country speaking to thousands of parents at baby and kids' expos, sharing my lunchbox tips and recipes. I am also proud to have been recently named an ambassador for the Jamie Oliver Learn Your Fruit & Veg Program.

People often tell my wife how lucky she is to have a husband who does the cooking and is so hands on. I don't see it that way. You see, I'm a parent; I'm just doing what a parent should do. Making school lunches isn't a 'mum' job, it's a 'parent' job. That's how I was brought up. After my dad passed away, we all had to pitch in, and the notion of 'men's work' and 'women's work' was something I never experienced.

I feel it's my duty to teach my girls the same lesson, to light their path so they can find their own way with confidence. I'm in a position to help them develop healthy expectations of how they should be treated by others. One way I do this is by making one-on-one time a priority, taking them out to do something special. I hope to help them build healthy self-esteem and learn to recognise when people don't treat them well.

I make lunches as an act of love for my girls (love in a lunchbox!) and I think that's what people respond to. I have included 30 of my most requested recipes in this book, as well as my tips and hacks for creating seriously good lunches that your kids will actually eat! I have also included snaps of lots of different bento-style lunchboxes to encourage and inspire you to create your own. I hope this book gives you the confidence to have a go at preparing healthy, colourful and fun meals for your kids (and yourself, too!). If I can do it, anyone can. So, let's get cooking!

THE WOMEN IN MY LIFE

There's the old saying that behind every great man is a great woman, but in my case, I stand behind the great women pictured here because they inspire me and help me to be the man that I am.

I was taught from a young age to treat women with the utmost respect. When I was a teenager, my father told me that when I approached girls, he wanted me to imagine how I'd want a guy to treat my sister, Suzy. This helped me to develop respect for all the girls in my life and has grown into a deep respect for all women. Today I want to support the goals and dreams of my wife, Marina, and our daughters, Anela and Kiki – I am their number-one supporter.

When I was a little boy, I loved to watch my mum cook. She would infuse simple ingredients with love, producing food for us that was so comforting and nourishing. Whenever I was in Mum's kitchen, I could forget all my troubles and relax, even though life was pretty tough at times. Mum's kitchen was a refuge, which I think is symbolic of the refuge *she* was, and still is, for all of us – the glue that holds us together.

Now I get to share my life with my incredible wife, Marina, whose hard work and dedication to our family and her own personal goals is inspiring to watch. I'm confident that Anela and Kiki will grow up knowing that they can achieve whatever they set their mind to because they have such an incredible role model in their mum.

I couldn't write this book without acknowledging the role these women play in my life. They are so much a part of me.

GETTING STARTED

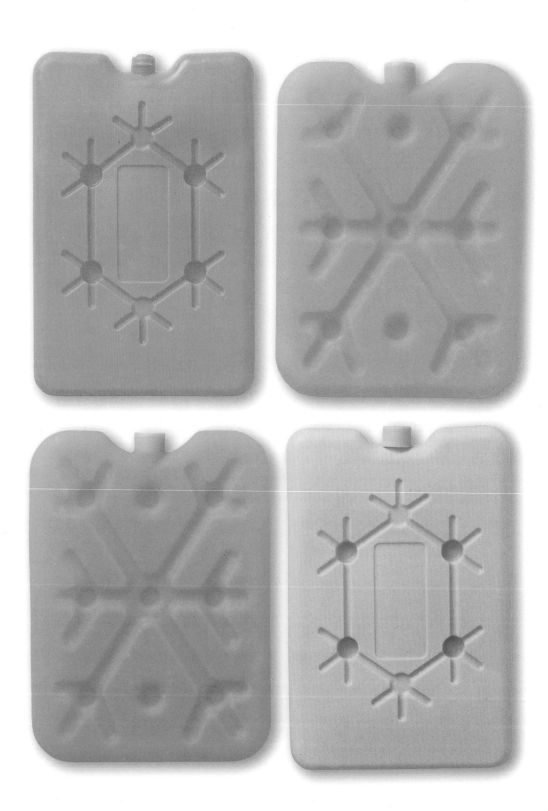

So you've picked up this book because you want to make fun, healthy, colourful lunches for your kids? Awesome, you're in the right place. Let me show you where to start when it comes to building a healthy lunch for your children, and also answer some of the most common questions I receive as the School Lunchbox Dad. I also share some of my lunch-making tricks and 'dad hacks', and my $50 shopping list that will enable you to make a week's worth of lunches for two kids.

MY LUNCHBOX PHILOSOPHY

Get familiar

Start using the lunchbox a month or so before your kid starts school. That way they'll be familiar with it by the time school rolls around and it won't be yet another new thing to get used to.

Have fun

Channel your inner creativity through your kids' lunchboxes! An interesting and varied lunchbox is fun for your kids, too, and means they're much more likely to eat what's inside.

Keep it balanced and healthy

In each lunchbox, I make sure there is a portion of protein, some veggies, dairy, fruit and a healthy treat. I prefer to include sugar-free treats, as I don't understand treats being automatically associated with sugar. Why reward your kids with something that's not good for them?

Stick to bite-sized portions

Kids are too busy to mess around with large portions – they just want to go and play. A mixture of bite-sized food is easier to grab and go.

Remember the number five

Make sure you include five fresh items (three veggies and two fruits) in every lunchbox – essential nutrition for growing bodies!

Eat the rainbow

Rainbows make my girls happy, so I put a rainbow in their lunchboxes every day. This not only looks appealing, but is a great way to ensure your kids are getting a wide variety of nutrients.

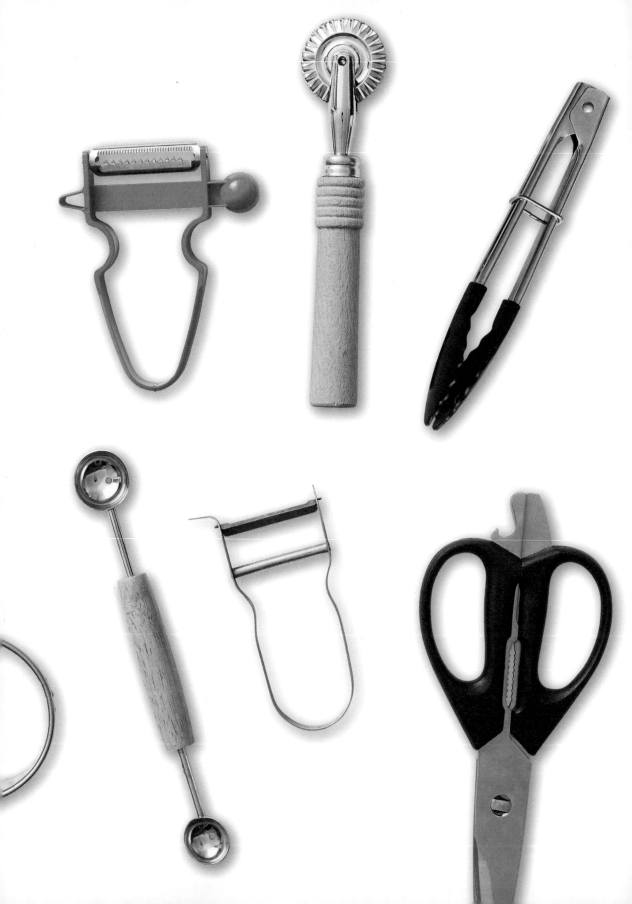

TOOLS OF THE TRADE

Bento lunchbox

I use bento-style lunchboxes. They're awesome as they don't leak, everything stays in the right place and the little sections make it easy to pack a balanced lunch. You can really use any type of lunchbox, using small containers to store the different lunch elements, but sometimes these are hard for little ones to manage.

Cooler bag

One of the most common questions I'm asked is how to keep lunches cool, especially when they contain meat and dairy. This is where the cooler bag comes in! You can use any type of cooler bag as long as it seals properly and fits the lunchbox and an ice pack.

Ice pack

These are really easy to pick up from most supermarkets. You could even make your own by freezing a bottle of water. Pop one in a cooler bag with the lunchbox and you can rest assured that your child's food will stay nice and cool.

Melon baller

I use one of these to create cute little bite-sized balls of fruit. I find my girls are more likely to eat fruit when it's presented in an interesting way, and this is a quick and easy trick to make fruit a bit more fun.

Protein shaker

A drink bottle with a screw-on lid, an internal mixer and a pouring spout, this will be your new best friend in the kitchen. I use it to make everything from pancakes to omelettes and cakes as it saves me from dirtying bowls, mixers and spoons. I reckon this is the ultimate tool for the lazy cook!

Ravioli cutter

You can find these in kitchenware shops or steal one from your mum's kitchen drawer (like I did! Sorry Ma!). I use my trusty ravioli cutter to make a number of things, such as my Rav-wich sandwich creations (see page 209).

Rolling pin

This is another kitchen essential that I use in a number of ways, the most common being to flatten out bread for my sandwich alternatives (see page 208). Any kind of rolling pin will do, even a wine bottle ... just make sure the lid is on tight!

Funnel

I like having a funnel handy to make filling the protein shaker a little less messy.

Veggie peeler

This is an essential tool in my kitchen. I use a standard peeler to make veggie ribbons (see Cu-shi Rolls on page 190) and a julienne peeler (see the red guy opposite) to grate carrots and make veggie noodles.

Chef's knife

You don't need to spend a fortune on a knife. I bought one of my favourite knives for $7 from an Asian grocer!

DAD HACKS, TIPS & TRICKS

Get a head start

I get up an hour before my girls do, make a pot of coffee and get myself ready for the day. Then I'm free to make my girls' lunches while they have breakfast and get ready.

Prep in advance

I like to be inspired in the moment when making lunches, but I still do some prep in advance to make life easier. I make sure all my fruit and veggies are washed, and then it's just a quick chop and assemble and we're good to go. I also make some things, such as Rob's Date & Coconut Bites (see page 166) and Mystery Puffs (see page 176), ahead of time.

Make it visually exciting

Picky eaters are more likely to try something new if it looks cool. And if you change up the presentation they never get bored. For example, I present sandwiches in so many different ways – check out page 208 for some ideas!

Keep it simple, stupid

Having said that, there's no need to go all out with works of art in your kids' lunchboxes. When I was looking for inspiration, I found so many things that were just way too complicated. Keep it fast, healthy and simple and you can't go wrong.

Be patient and persistent

Both of my kids are picky in different ways, and sometimes one of the six bento box compartments will come home untouched. I call the uneaten item – which is usually something new – 'the risk taker'. I'll try the risk taker again the following week and then again the week after. Getting kids used to new foods is a gradual process.

Get the kids involved

Whether it's cooking, prepping, assembling or even choosing their own fruit at the supermarket, the more I get my girls involved the more they embrace their lunches. They love helping me come up with fun names for my creations, too.

Make it educational

I love teaching my kids about different cultures and countries through food. Check out the International Fridays section (see page 121) for inspiration!

THE $50 SHOPPING LIST: IS IT POSSIBLE?

I have put together a $50 shopping list that will cover two children's school lunches for one week. It works out to $5 per lunch per child. I know if I fine-tuned it further by shopping around I'd probably be able to get the cost down even lower, but the reality is you don't want to be driving all over town with kids in tow to save $5 or $10 – you want to get all your shopping done in the one place.

You can make some excellent lunches with the ingredients on this list. I have even included blueberries, croissants and wraps! The key is to be creative with what you have. These prices are based on a shop I did at a major supermarket, and are current as of January 2019. Prices may vary according to the season. It was summer when I shopped, so blueberries were cheap. Feel free to use whatever fruit is in season and most affordable.

1 punnet grape tomatoes	$3.50
1 avocado	$3.00
1 kg carrots, pre-packed	$1.50
1 punnet blueberries	$3.50
½ seedless watermelon	$4.00
1 punnet strawberries	$3.00
2 Lebanese cucumbers	$1.26
1 kg granny smith apples, pre-packed	$4.80
1 head broccoli	$2.04
2 bananas	$1.08
1 bag (700 g) shredded tasty cheese	$5.80
125 g deli sliced triple-smoked leg ham	$3.13
125 g deli sliced chicken loaf	$1.56
12 large free-range eggs (1 carton)	$4.60
8 pack wholemeal & grain soft wraps	$2.25
4 pack croissants	$2.50
1 loaf home brand white bread	$1.25
TOTAL	**$48.77**

THINGS TO DO WITH
BREAD & WRAP OFFCUTS
(AND UNEATEN PIZZA CRUSTS!)

Store bread offcuts in reusable containers or zip-lock bags in the freezer for up to 3 months.

Make croutons by cutting bread offcuts into small cubes and toasting them under the grill until golden brown.

Make a simple stuffing mix for chicken by blending up bread offcuts with 1 finely chopped onion, 1 teaspoon of mixed herbs, 1 egg, 2 tablespoons of butter and a little salt and pepper.

Make breadcrumbs by blending up bread offcuts. These can be stored in an airtight container and frozen for up to 3 months.

Make one of my bread-based creations, such as Banana Bread Balls (see page 164) or Apple and Blueberry Br-uffins (see page 172).

30 DAYS OF KIDS' LUNCHBOXES

When I was a kid, I was often sent to school with traditional Macedonian food in my lunchbox. I was embarrassed because the other kids had simple 'Aussie' lunches, such as Vegemite sandwiches on white bread, packets of chips and juice boxes. Now I look back and realise how lucky I was to have a mum who sent me to school with such delicious food. In this chapter, I have put together 30 different bento-style lunchboxes to show you my lunch-building formula in action and hopefully inspire you to get creative, too. Boring lunches begone!

Make lunches colourful and fun!

LOW-SALT PRETZELS ARE ALWAYS ON HAND IN OUR PANTRY.

A squeeze of lemon juice will keep fruit slices from browning.

There are so many variations of bread sticks. Try tiger bread for something different!

Keep things bite-sized!

Leave grapes on the stem for a sense of fun.

Popcorn is quick to make in the morning or easy to buy in bulk.

Plain yoghurt is a good dip option for veggies and fruit.

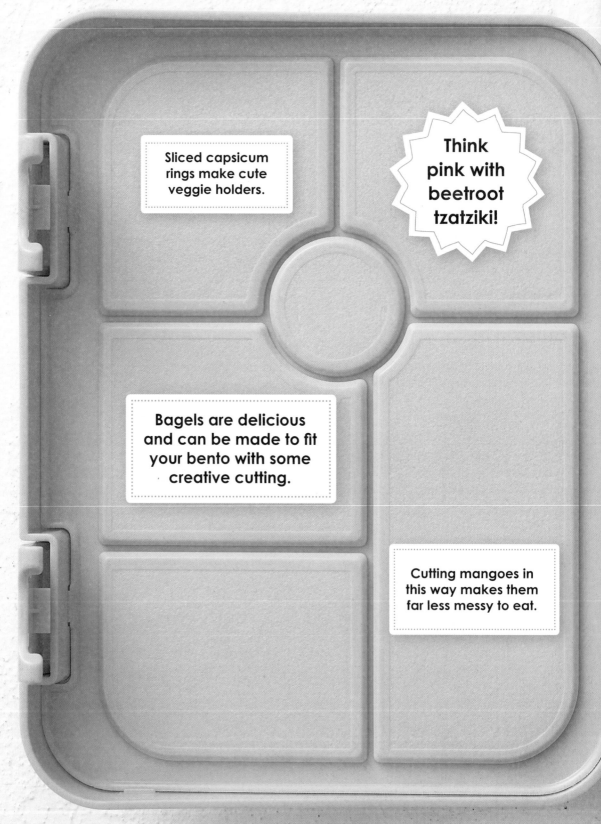

Sliced capsicum rings make cute veggie holders.

Think pink with beetroot tzatziki!

Bagels are delicious and can be made to fit your bento with some creative cutting.

Cutting mangoes in this way makes them far less messy to eat.

Make the most of dinner leftovers!

Fresh or frozen, berries are perfect lunchbox additions.

Drizzle pasta with a little olive oil to stop it going sticky or soggy.

Blanch veggies to preserve their flavour and texture.

Buy a dozen little bread rolls and freeze them. Take them out to thaw the night before as you need them.

Pre-cut fruit makes life easy!

Change up the veggies you include in your kids' lunchboxes regularly. Is there anything cuter than baby corn?

I don't always have a chip on my shoulder, but when I do, I'm going to eat it.

Keep it fast and fresh!

Make your own bread twists with leftover pizza dough.

Melon ballers make fruit so fun! So does presenting it like this.

RAV-WICH, SEE PAGE 209.

A squeeze of lime over dragon fruit adds a whole new dimension.

If it's pretty they will eat!

A mix of sliced and whole fruit and veg keeps things interesting.

SAND-LING, SEE PAGE 209.

Sand-ling won't stick? Microwave the bread for 4–5 seconds first.

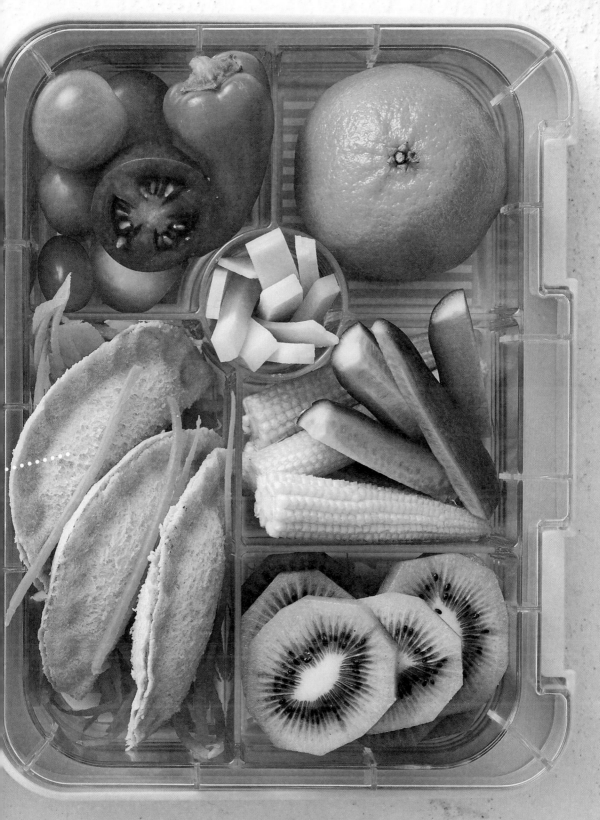

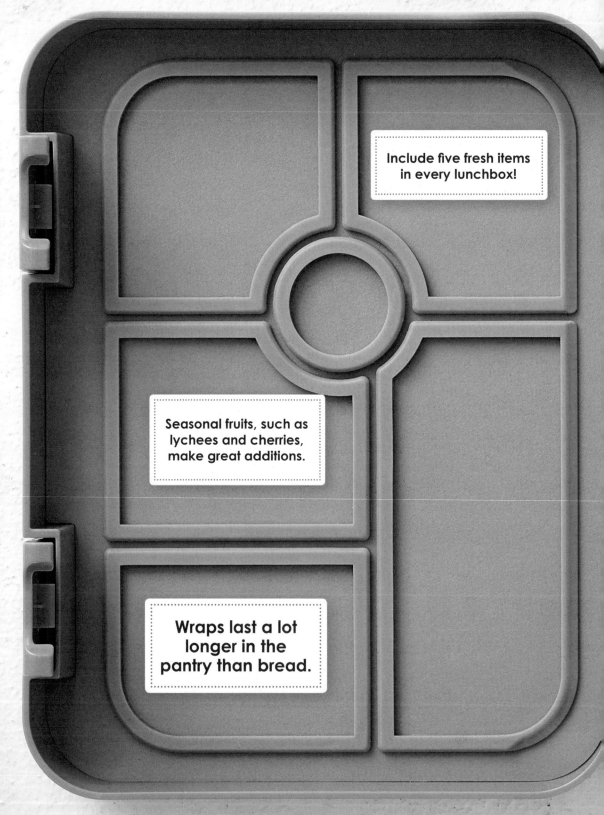

Include five fresh items in every lunchbox!

Seasonal fruits, such as lychees and cherries, make great additions.

Wraps last a lot longer in the pantry than bread.

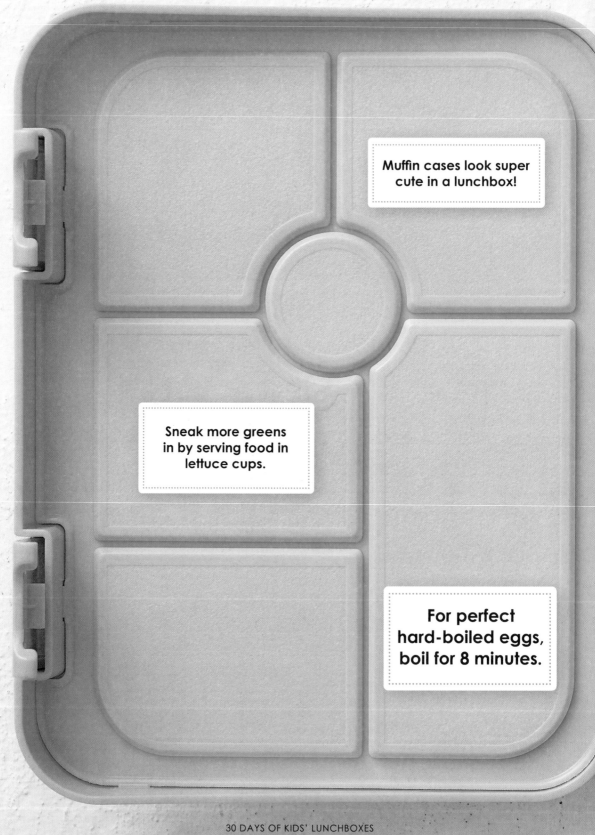

Muffin cases look super cute in a lunchbox!

Sneak more greens in by serving food in lettuce cups.

For perfect hard-boiled eggs, boil for 8 minutes.

Pesto is always
a great addition!

Spring-wiches (and
their cousins, see
page 208) are great
ways to hide veggies.

SPRING-WICH,
SEE PAGE 209.

Sweet bell peppers are
fun and bright additions!

Grissini with
a tasty dip make
a great snack.

VEGETABLE
DOUGHNUTS,
SEE PAGE 182.

My friend asked me, 'What rhymes with orange?'

I laughed at him and said, 'No it doesn't.'

Deli-sliced chicken loaf or ham with cheese and salad is my go-to for wraps.

Express your love in a lunchbox!

Use cookie cutters to create a masterpiece.

Get adventurous with different types of wraps, such as seeded, garlic, etc.

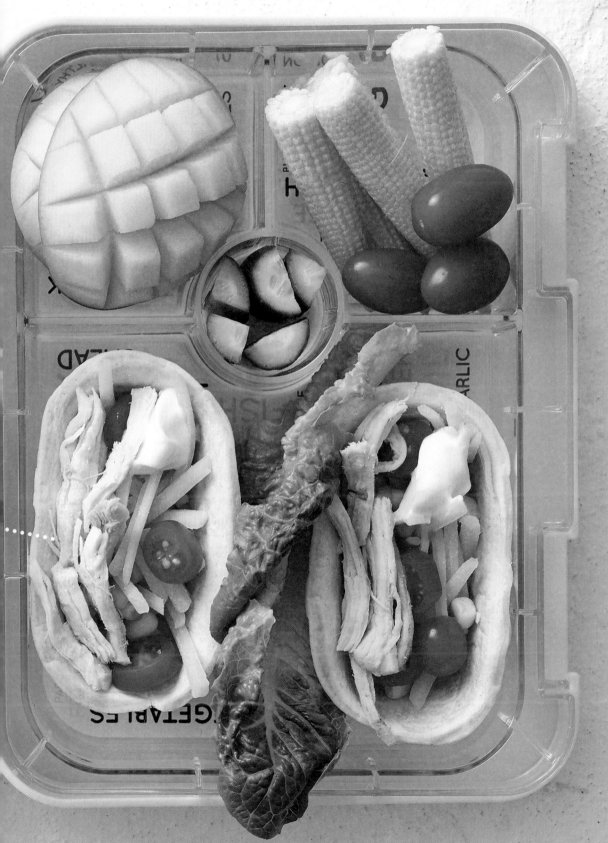

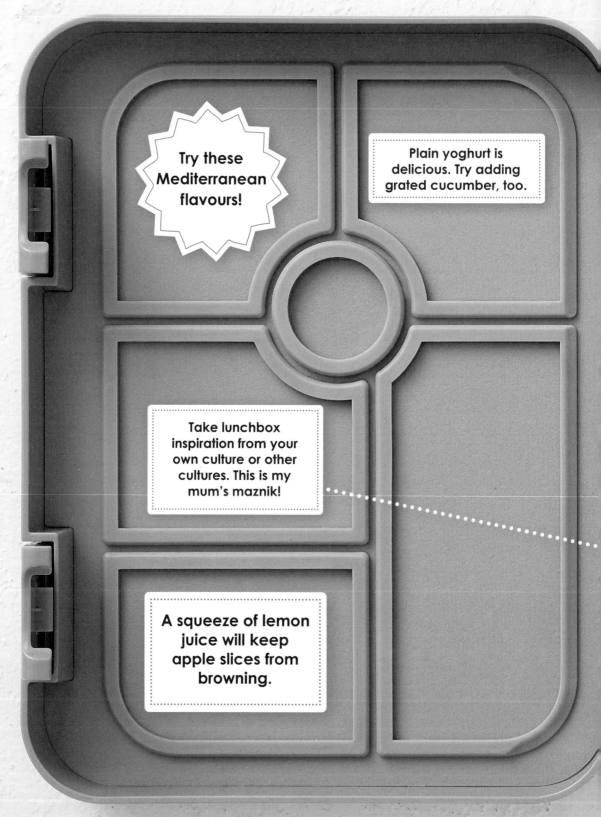

Try these Mediterranean flavours!

Plain yoghurt is delicious. Try adding grated cucumber, too.

Take lunchbox inspiration from your own culture or other cultures. This is my mum's maznik!

A squeeze of lemon juice will keep apple slices from browning.

Capsicum cups make great edible containers!

You CAN occasionally let your kids peel their own fruit. Make them work for it …

FETA CHEESE IS A TASTY SOURCE OF PROTEIN.

Fresh is always best!

Try lightly toasting vol-au-vents and stuffing with egg or tuna. Yum!

ALWAYS BUY PRETZELS AND CRACKERS IN BULK.

Remember to deseed your kids' olives.

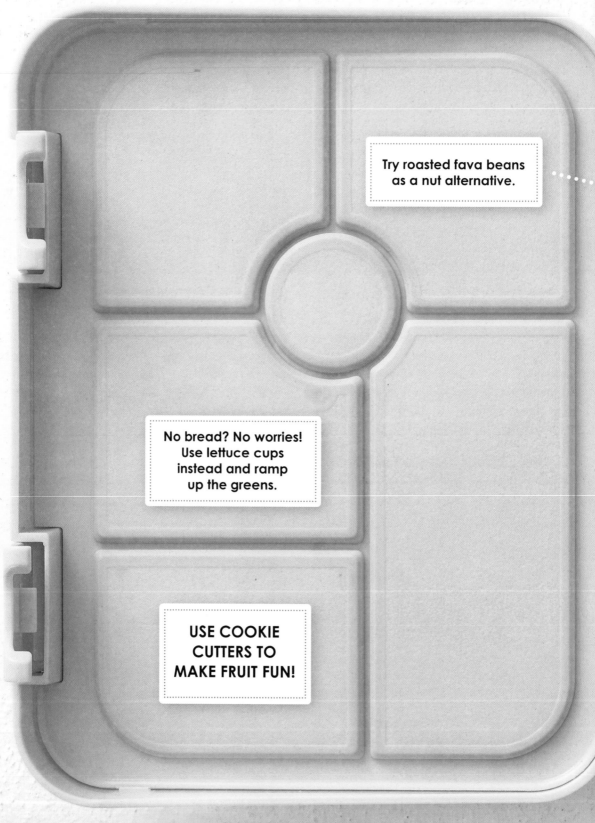

Try roasted fava beans as a nut alternative.

No bread? No worries! Use lettuce cups instead and ramp up the greens.

USE COOKIE CUTTERS TO MAKE FRUIT FUN!

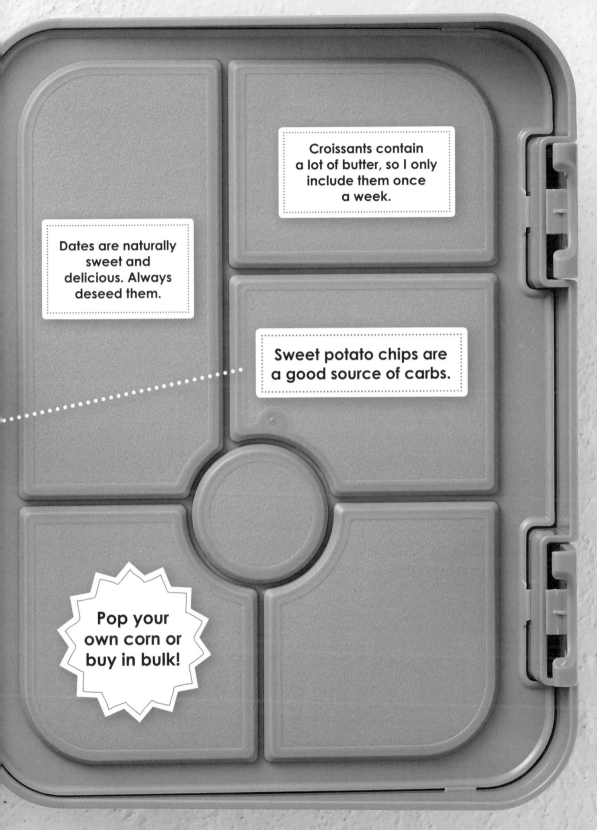

Croissants contain a lot of butter, so I only include them once a week.

Dates are naturally sweet and delicious. Always deseed them.

Sweet potato chips are a good source of carbs.

Pop your own corn or buy in bulk!

My wife gets annoyed if I mess with her red wine, so I added fruit and lemonade to it and now she's sangria than ever!

It only
takes five
minutes!

Making your own
hummus is easy.
Google it.

Look for alternatives
to traditional bread like
these wholemeal thins.

Brighten things up by using all three capsicum colours!

Pestos and dips are a great way for your kids to try new flavours.

TACO TUGBOATS, SEE PAGE 206.

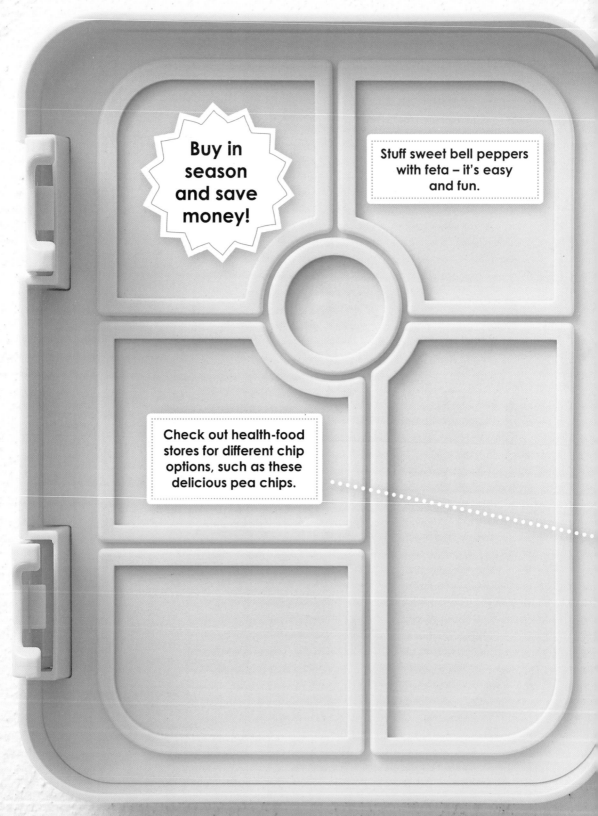

Buy in season and save money!

Stuff sweet bell peppers with feta – it's easy and fun.

Check out health-food stores for different chip options, such as these delicious pea chips.

Get creative, have fun!

Don't buy individually wrapped cheese slices. Save on packaging and cut from a family-sized block.

BLUEBERRIES ARE SO GOOD FOR US.

Ham and chicken wraps? Yes please!

Let the kids fill their own pita pockets. It gives them a sense of achievement!

Add a teaspoon of mayo to canned tuna so it doesn't dry out.

GIVE FRUIT A QUICK WASH FIRST.

Make mini soft-shell tacos out of wraps using a cookie cutter.

REPLACE SOUR CREAM WITH PLAIN YOGHURT.

Qukes (yes, mini cucumbers) are fun and bite-sized.

Create your own salsa and serve it in the avo shell!

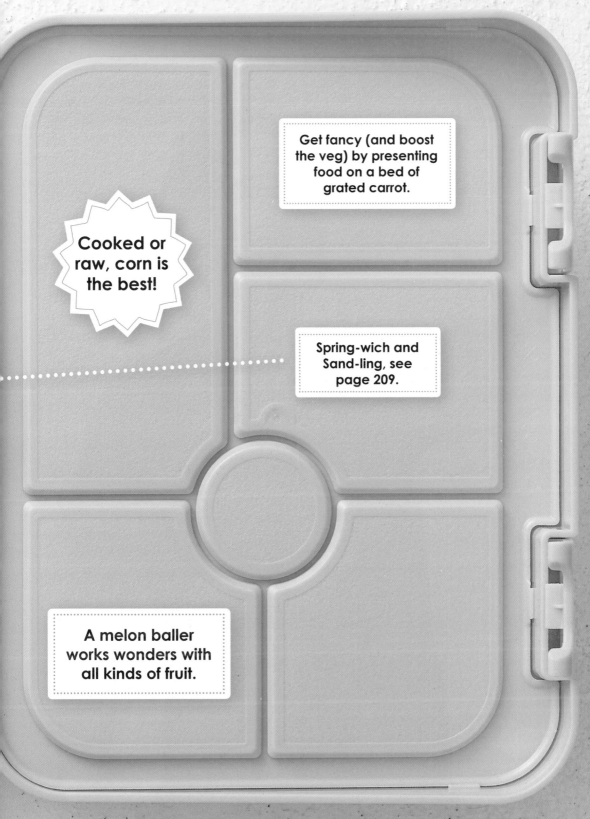

Get fancy (and boost the veg) by presenting food on a bed of grated carrot.

Cooked or raw, corn is the best!

Spring-wich and Sand-ling, see page 209.

A melon baller works wonders with all kinds of fruit.

Always eat the rainbow!

Mashed avo with a squeeze of lemon makes a great dip.

Keep an eye out for fun cracker shapes to mix things up.

Pre-bought sushi rolls are great when you're running low on time.

Always cut the sharp ends off any skewers!

When packing meat or seafood, pop the lunchbox in a cooler bag with an ice pack.

APPLE ROSES, SEE PAGE 168.

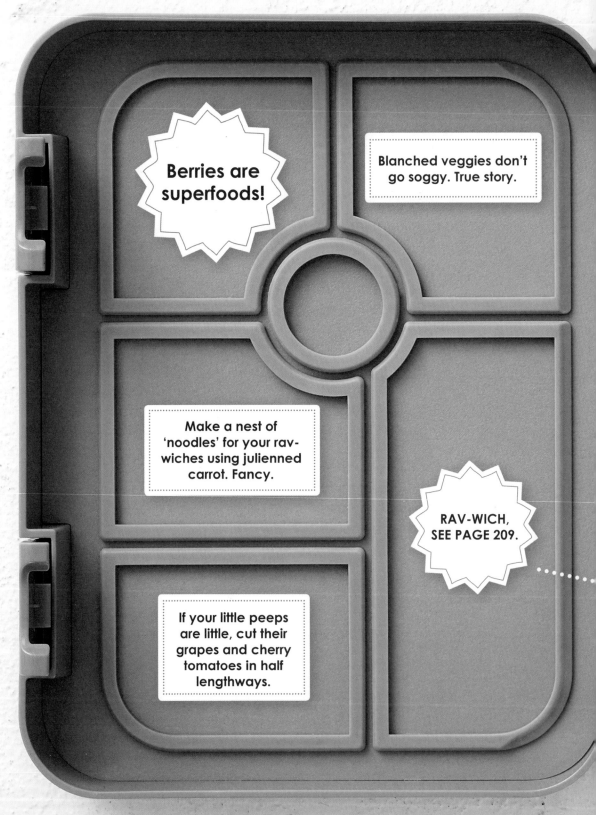

Berries are superfoods!

Blanched veggies don't go soggy. True story.

Make a nest of 'noodles' for your rav-wiches using julienned carrot. Fancy.

RAV-WICH, SEE PAGE 209.

If your little peeps are little, cut their grapes and cherry tomatoes in half lengthways.

Dips are often on sale and they keep well in the fridge.

English muffins always go down well!

Low-salt or salt-free popcorn makes a healthy snack.

Veggie chips rock! Try making your own to avoid preservatives.

BONUS ADULT LUNCHBOXES

Why should kids have all the fun? It's important to take care of ourselves as parents, too, to give us the energy we need to take care of our little humans. Once I realised how awesome bento-style lunchboxes were, I decided to buy my own and create some 'grown-up' lunches. The basics of building adult lunches are the same – protein such as chicken, healthy carbs like brown rice, veggies, some dairy and a little fruit – I just increase the portion sizes a little bit. I don't always include every element, but it's a good mental checklist to have when thinking about what to eat for the day. I hope you enjoy these lunchbox ideas!

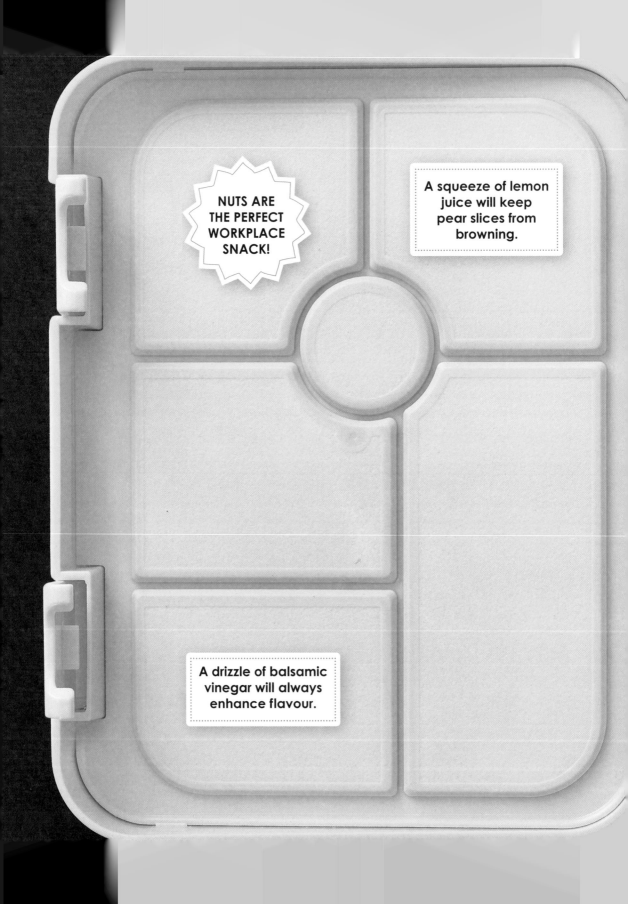

NUTS ARE THE PERFECT WORKPLACE SNACK!

A squeeze of lemon juice will keep pear slices from browning.

A drizzle of balsamic vinegar will always enhance flavour.

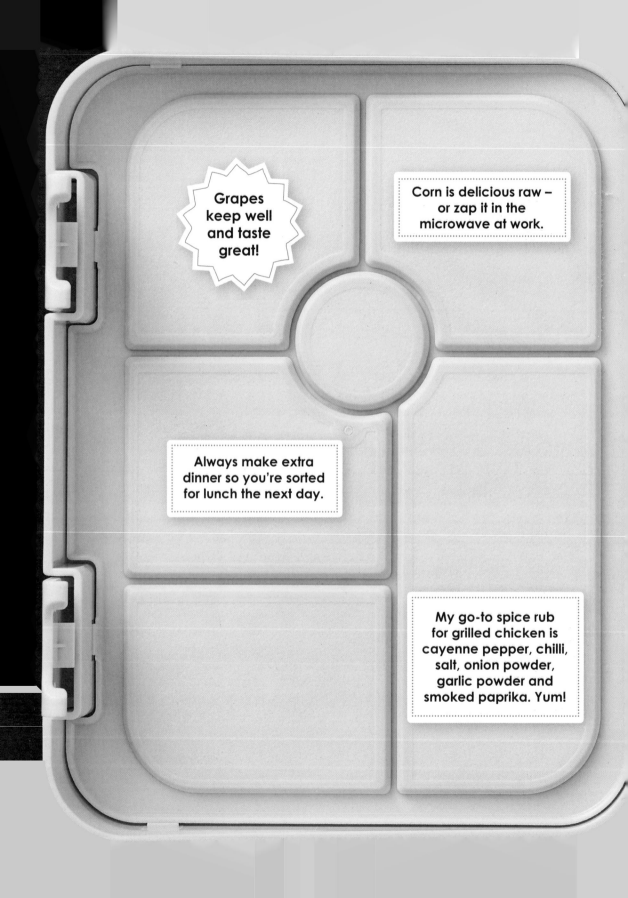

Dragon fruit and fresh lime juice are a match made in heaven.

Make it colourful and fun!

Lettuce cups mean less mess at the desk. We've all been there ...

Try using black rice – it's delicious!

I was going to take
a new job where they paid me
in vegetables, but the celery
was unacceptable.

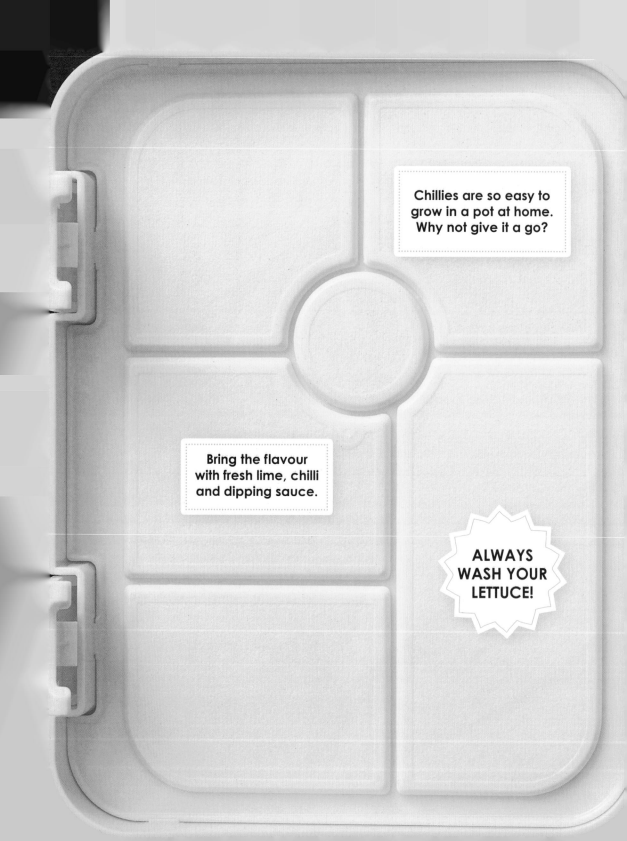

You can't beat seasonal fruit like cherries!

A whole roast chicken from the supermarket is a cheap way to fill many lunchboxes.

Brighten up leftovers with some fresh additions.

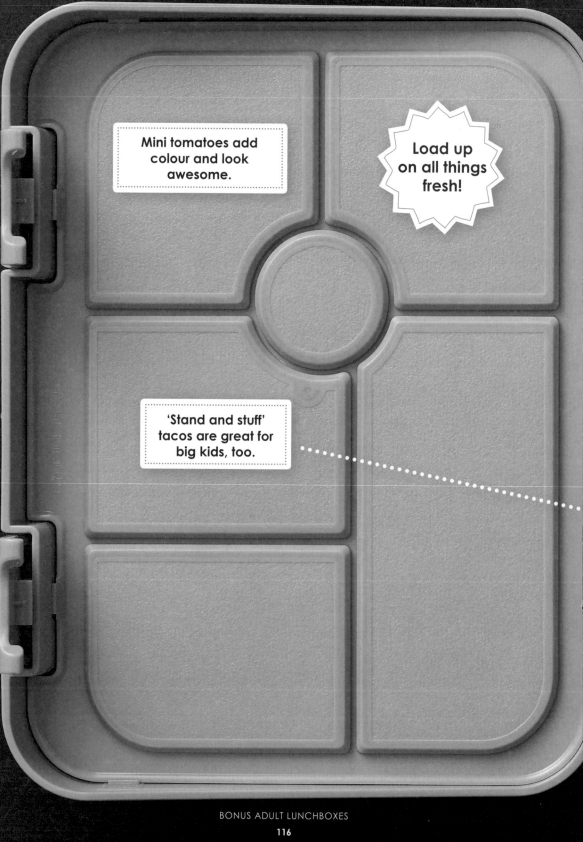

Mini tomatoes add colour and look awesome.

Load up on all things fresh!

'Stand and stuff' tacos are great for big kids, too.

Blanching veggies
for 30–45 seconds
gives them crunch
and flavour.

WHO
DOESN'T LOVE
A PRAWN
CRACKER?

Leftover takeaway
makes the perfect
work lunch.

INTERNATIONAL
FRIDAYS

I started International or 'Heritage' Fridays as a way of helping my girls to see themselves as citizens of the world. I realised that the information they were getting about other countries and cultures in the media wasn't always showing the whole picture. So I thought, what better way to educate them than by packing lunchboxes showcasing foods and fun facts about different places around the globe? Through researching each featured country, I also learned a lot, so I encourage you to do the same. Here are just a few countries to get you going.

UK

The UK's capital city is London.

The UK is made up of four countries: England, Scotland, Wales and Northern Ireland.

LONDON WAS FOUNDED ALMOST 2,000 YEARS AGO BY THE ROMANS.

The UK has a population of 66 million people.

Queen Elizabeth II is the queen of England. She has ruled for 67 years!

British inventions include the telescope, tin can and photography.

ITALY

Rome is Italy's capital city.

Famous artists Leonardo da Vinci, Michelangelo and Sandro Botticelli all came from Italy.

ITALIANS INVENTED THE BAROMETER AND PIANO!

Italy has a population of 61 million people.

Tomatoes didn't arrive in Italy until the 16th century. Can you imagine pasta sauce without tomatoes?

The Pope lives in the Vatican City, a tiny country within Rome!

Japan's capital city is Tokyo.

Pokémon, Hello Kitty, Sailor Moon and Totoro all come from Japan!

WASABI

JAPAN

'KAWAII' MEANS CUTE IN JAPANESE.

Japan has a population of 126 million people.

Japan's national sport is sumo wrestling, but baseball is the most popular.

Tokyo will host the 2020 Olympic Games.

Lake Ohrid in southwest Macedonia is one of Europe's oldest and deepest lakes.

Skopje is Macedonia's capital city.

MACEDONIA

Mother Teresa was born in Skopje in 1910.

Darko Pančev and Goran Pandev are famous Macedonian soccer players!

Milcho Manchevski is an award-winning Macedonian film director.

MEXICO

Mexico City is the capital – easy!

Although most Mexicans speak Spanish, there are 68 official languages.

MEXICO IS THE SIXTH MOST-VISITED COUNTRY.

Mexico has a population of 129 million people.

Chocolate (cacao) comes from Mexico and was used as currency by the Aztecs. (I'd eat all my currency!)

Avocados, tomatoes, chillies, corn, coriander and vanilla all come from Mexico.

POLAND

Ninety per cent of Poles finish high school, which may explain why Poland has produced 17 Nobel Prize winners!

POPE JOHN PAUL II WAS FROM POLAND.

Poland's capital city is Warsaw.

Krystyna Chojnowska-Liskiewicz was the first woman to sail solo around the world!

Polska

Poland has a population of 38.5 million people.

The Warner Bros. were originally from Poland.

SWITZERLAND

The Swiss capital city is Bern.

German, French, Italian and Romansh are the official languages.

TENNIS STAR ROGER FEDERER IS SWISS!

The Red Cross was founded in Switzerland and based its symbol on the Swiss flag.

The Swiss population is 8.5 million people.

I wouldn't really put this much chocolate in my kid's lunchbox, guys ...

THAILAND

The Thai capital is Bangkok.

The population of Thailand is 68 million people.

Thai food is based around five key flavours: sweet, spicy, sour, bitter and salty.

THE ELEPHANT IS THAILAND'S NATIONAL SYMBOL.

Thailand's signature sport is Muay Thai, a form of kickboxing!

The majority of Thai people are Buddhist.

Twenty-one of the 100 tallest buildings in the world are located in the UAE.

The UAE has more than 44 million date palms, producing 76,000 tonnes of dates every year!

The USA has a population of 326 million people.

The capital city is Washington DC.

USA

Although Christopher Columbus is often credited with discovering America in 1492, Native American Indians were the original owners – respect!

THE BALD EAGLE IS THE NATIONAL SYMBOL OF THE USA.

Thanksgiving Day is celebrated every year on the fourth Thursday in November.

The US flag has 50 stars – one to represent each state!

RECIPES

I'm all about the quick assembly when it comes to making lunchboxes in the morning, so I always like to have a couple of items prepared in advance, such as muffins, pastries and energy balls. Set aside a bit of time on the weekend to whip up some of these simple recipes and your kids will love you for it! Having said that, most of my recipes are so quick to prepare that you could actually make them in the morning … if you can stop yourself hitting that snooze button. I hope you and your kids enjoy these simple, tasty ideas.

BANANA & CORNFLAKE BREAKFAST MUFFINS

Makes 6

I set myself a challenge to make breakfast cool again, but more importantly, I wanted to stop those overripe bananas in the fruit bowl going to waste. Cornflakes are one of the most iconic breakfast cereals, so I thought why not combine bananas and cornflakes in the form of a muffin? Not only do I get to use up those bananas, but I also create a breakfast that can be eaten on the run if need be. Who else can say they had banana and cornflakes in the car on their way to school?

olive oil, for greasing

4 ripe bananas, 1 sliced

½ cup self-raising flour

1 egg

2 tablespoons honey, plus extra for drizzling

1 cup cornflakes (or oats or other cereal)

1. Preheat the oven to 170°C. Lightly grease a six-hole muffin tin. In a mixing bowl, use a fork to mash the three whole bananas until fairly smooth (a few lumps are okay).

2. Add the rest of the ingredients (except the sliced banana) and, using the fork, mix everything together until nicely combined. My wife prefers to use a spatula for the mixing, but considering you've already dirtied a fork from mashing the bananas, I just use that instead, as it's less for me to wash up.

3. Spoon the mixture evenly into the prepared muffin holes until they are three-quarters full (remember the self-raising flour will make the muffins rise, so you don't want to fill them all the way to the top).

4. Arrange some of the sliced banana on top of the muffin batter. Drizzle some extra honey over the top and pop the tin in the oven for 18–20 minutes. Once cooked, enjoy them warm or put them in an airtight container and store in the fridge for up to 4 days or freezer for up to 3 months. To reheat, zap them in the microwave for 30 seconds.

TIP Try using a handful of blueberries instead of bananas or, even better, try using both!

CINNAMON & HONEY SCROLLS

Makes 6

Have I mentioned how much I love the versatility of puff pastry from the freezer? It's awesome. With this creation, I wanted to make a tasty no-refined-sugar school lunchbox addition. For grown-ups, they're delightful with a nice latte or double-shot espresso, or even an espresso martini ... Cinnamon has fantastic characteristics, the best being that it's surprisingly sweet. In my little family we treat cinnamon as a sugar alternative and it rocks!

1 sheet of frozen puff pastry, thawed

2 teaspoons ground cinnamon

3 tablespoons honey

 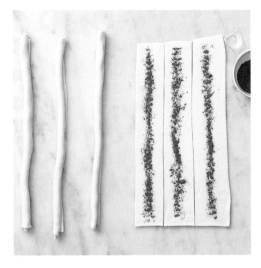

1. Preheat the oven to 180°C. Line a baking tray with baking paper. Cut the pastry into six 3 cm-wide strips. You don't need to get the ruler out; it really doesn't matter if they're not perfect. Now sprinkle three-quarters of the cinnamon somewhat consistently over the top.

2. Using the palms of your hands, roll the pastry strips into long snakes, making sure they are nice and tight.

3. Now coil each pastry snake to create a snail effect or round shape. They should be about 5 cm in diameter. Place on the prepared tray and drizzle the honey over the top of the scrolls.

4. Sprinkle the scrolls with the remaining cinnamon and pop them in the oven for about 20 minutes until puffed up and cooked through. If you don't eat them straight away, the scrolls will keep in an airtight container for 4–5 days.

 TIPS Feel free to add more cinnamon or honey for a sweeter scroll.
Apart from being delicious, they're also guilt-free without added refined sugar, but don't tell your friends (otherwise there won't be as many left for you).

BERRY GOOD PUFF-CAKES

Makes 6

I love cupcakes and I love puff pastry from the freezer, so why not combine
the two to create a 'berry good puff-cake'? I like to keep things simple, and
I especially like it when a treat is so easy to make that I can whip it up during
a commercial break. Not that I watch *The Bachelor* or anything ...

When you see frozen puff pastry on sale at the supermarket, don't question it,
just load up. I love how quickly it thaws, as it means you can get on with cooking
straight away. So, check out this next little creation. What? Just four ingredients?
This is going to be easy.

olive oil, for greasing

1 sheet of frozen puff pastry, thawed

1 cup hulled strawberries

¾ cup blueberries (or any fruit except citrus)

1. Preheat the oven to 180°C and lightly grease a six-hole muffin tin. Lay the pastry sheet on top of the muffin tin. Being careful not to tear the pastry, gently press it down into each hole until you can touch the base of the tin.

2. Fill each hole with strawberries and blueberries and, using a pasta cutter, pizza cutter or a knife, cut the pastry into squares around each muffin hole.

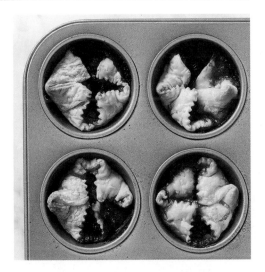

3. Fold the corners of each pastry square into the centre. Not all the berries will be covered but that's okay, as the berry juice will overflow and the puff-cakes will look rustic and colourful.

4. Pop them in the oven and bake for 20–25 minutes or until the pastry is golden brown. Let the puff-cakes cool for 5 minutes, as you'll burn your tongue if you don't wait (you just did, didn't you?). If there are any leftovers, the puff-cakes will keep in an airtight container for 3–4 days.

TIP If you need to impress the in-laws just sprinkle a little icing sugar on top.

HOT JAM DOUGHNUTS

Makes 4

Hot jam doughnuts? Say no more. Is there anything more satisfying on
a cold day, or any day for that matter? I wanted to figure out a way to make
doughnuts for my girls to enjoy, but without as much sugar. So, while having
fun in the kitchen one morning I decided to get creative with the simplest of
ingredients. I even popped them in a brown bag to replicate the doughnut van
experience, plus it saved me from washing more dishes. Fold the corner of this
page because you'll love this recipe. Note: If you decide to take a photograph
of your doughnuts, make sure you don't eat them before the photo is taken ...
like I did when shooting this recipe ... whoops!

½ cup strawberry jam (or any jam you
have on hand)

8 slices of wholemeal bread

2 tablespoons butter

ground cinnamon, for sprinkling

caster sugar, for sprinkling (optional if you
think the jam is sweet enough)

1. Spoon 1 tablespoon of jam into the centre of four slices of bread. (If you don't drip jam on yourself later while eating these, you clearly haven't added enough filling.)

2. Pop a slice of bread on top of one, then, using an upside-down coffee mug, push down hard until the surrounding part of the bread comes away and the edges are sealed. Carefully remove the bread from the mug and repeat the process to make four doughnuts.

3. Melt the butter in a frying pan over medium heat. Sprinkle some cinnamon into the pan, so it caramelises and infuses the butter. Place your doughnuts in the frying pan and, using tongs, move them around the pan to coat them in the butter and cinnamon. Flip them over and let the doughnuts toast a little further. The smell at this stage will be heavenly.

4. Remove the doughnuts from the pan, lightly sprinkle over some more cinnamon and a little caster sugar (if using) and enjoy.

TIP You can also use a cookie cutter to create fun shapes.

I was washing my car with my daughter the other day and she asked, 'Dad, why don't you just use a sponge?'

DAD-STYLE PIKELETS

Serves 3

Sunday morning pikelets are a ritual at my place. I remember years ago buying the packet mix and using that, but it lacked soul and was too expensive. Then I researched a few recipes but found them to be too messy, and washing up kind of sucks. So, I decided to make my own dad-style pikelets. This was my first ever creation using a protein shaker and it had a huge response on my social media pages, so I had to include it here to hopefully revive or maybe even start the Sunday morning pikelet ritual for you. If you can resist eating the pikelets while cooking them, please let me know your secret.

1 cup milk (use soy, almond or lactose-free milk if you prefer)

1 egg

3 tablespoons maple syrup or honey, plus extra for drizzling

1 cup self-raising flour

oil spray or knob of butter (optional)

6–9 strawberries, chopped (or use any fruit you like instead of strawberries and blueberries – imagine caramelising some apples and adding cinnamon!)

½ cup blueberries

1. Heat a shallow non-stick frying pan over low heat. Add the milk, egg and maple syrup or honey to the protein shaker, followed by the flour. Screw the lid on and shake it for about 1 minute to mix. Don't stress too much if it's not silky smooth – just call them rustic pikelets if the mixture's a bit lumpy.

2. Depending on how non-stick your frying pan is, spray it with some olive oil or add a little butter. Open up the protein shaker and pour a 3 cm round of the mixture into the frying pan. Keep doing this until you've filled the pan.

3. After a minute or so, use a wooden skewer to start flipping the pikelets, making sure the undersides are golden brown first. Cook for a further minute, then remove to a plate. Remember to eat the first one; this is called taste-testing. Repeat with the remaining batter.

4. I love to stack 7–9 pikelets on top of each other, then top with the strawberries and blueberries and finish with a drizzle of maple syrup or honey. So damn good! These pikelets will be a guaranteed hit, plus you can refrigerate or freeze any leftovers for the following Sunday. Reheating them in the microwave only takes a few seconds.

 TIP Cleaning up has never been so easy! Just fill the protein shaker with warm water and soap and hope that someone else cleans it later.

SHAKIN' BLUEBERRY MUFFINS

Makes 6

We all love muffins. We see them in cafes when ordering our takeaway coffees and get tempted. I know what it's like. So, I thought I'd make my own 'dad' version of the blueberry muffin using the protein shaker. This recipe is so quick you can even make it in between your favourite TV shows. Some of you might be tempted to add choc chips instead of blueberries, which is okay because they kind of look like blueberries anyway. If you do use blueberries, avoid using the frozen ones, as they make the muffins go soggy. Stick to the fresh stuff. These muffins were voted 'the best muffins ever created' by my mum, who'd had a couple of Champagnes at the time.

butter, for greasing

¾ cup milk (use soy, almond or lactose-free milk if you prefer)

1 egg

¼ cup vegetable oil, plus extra for greasing

1 tablespoon sugar (or use cinnamon or maple syrup if you like)

½ cup blueberries, plus extra for decorating (or use strawberries or any other berry you like)

1 cup self-raising flour

1. Preheat the oven to 180°C and grease a six-hole muffin tin. Twist open the lid of your protein shaker and add the ingredients, finishing with the self-raising flour. Close the lid and give it a good shake.

2. After 1 minute of shaking, grab your muffin tin and pour the muffin mixture into the greased holes until they are three-quarters full.

3. Decorate the tops with a few extra blueberries and pop the tin in the oven for 20–25 minutes.

4. Once they're cooked, I guarantee you'll eat at least one before the kids even see them. You can always tell the kids you dropped one and the dog ate it. If you don't have a dog, buy one for this reason alone. You'll thank me later.

 TIP The muffins will keep in an airtight container in the fridge for up to 4 days or in the freezer for up to 3 months. Reheat them in the microwave or enjoy them cold; they're delicious either way.

BANANA BREAD BALLS

Makes 11

A while ago, I was flicking through a cookbook looking for a banana bread recipe. I almost fell over when I saw the number of ingredients and steps it took to make it. The title certainly fooled me, as I presumed the recipe would be just banana, bread and a sweetener. So here is my version of banana bread with, you guessed it, banana, bread and a sweetener. If the simple things in life are the best, then let's keep them simple.

5 slices of wholemeal bread (or 5 cups roughly chopped bread offcuts. Use any bread you like – gluten-free bread works well, too)

2 bananas

2 teaspoons ground cinnamon

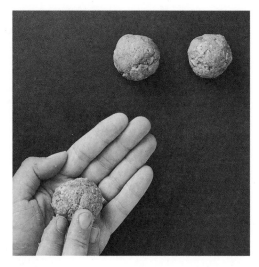

1. Preheat the oven to 175°C or an air-fryer on medium heat. Pop the ingredients in a blender. Wait, what? That's it? You got it. Power up the blender and let it do its magic for 20–30 seconds.

2. Take the lid off and transfer the mixture to a bowl. Grab a tablespoon of the mixture and roll it into a solid ball (this is a fun bit for the kids to help with).

3. Repeat the rolling process until you've used all the mixture. You should have around 11 balls.

4. Pop the banana bread balls on a greased tray and bake in the oven for 10 minutes or drop them into the air-fryer for 5 minutes. Enjoy straight away or store in the fridge for up to 5 days.

 TIPS Try adding additional ingredients, such as blueberries – delicious!
Also try not to eat them all while they're still warm.

ROB'S DATE & COCONUT BITES

Makes 9

I love dates, especially the Persian variety. Just add desiccated coconut and you have something pretty damn tasty. This recipe was inspired by my Persian refugee friend Rahoulla (Rob for short). He would always bring Persian dates as a gift when he visited us. We ended up with so many that I decided to create something delicious with them to stop our pantry overflowing. So, I pulled out the trusted blender, added some desiccated coconut and we made this awesome two-ingredient treat.

10 dates, pitted (or use dried apricots, which are just as yummy but don't help if your pantry is, like mine, full of dates)

⅓ cup desiccated coconut, plus extra for rolling

1. Place the dates and desiccated coconut in a blender and blitz until everything looks mushy and really sticky.

2. Transfer the mixture to a bowl and roll teaspoons of the mixture into nine balls.

3. Roll the balls in a heap of desiccated coconut and ensure they're evenly coated – the idea is for all the stickiness to be covered by the coconut.

4. Pop them in the fridge for 1 hour until set. Afterwards, make yourself a cup of coffee, put your feet up and eat them all; there's no way the kids are getting any once you realise just how easy to make and delicious they are. If there are any leftovers, they make an excellent treat to pop in school lunchboxes, as they contain no added sugar.

 TIPS Try adding a little cocoa powder for a chocolaty taste.

These keep well in an airtight container in the freezer for up to 3 months.

APPLE ROSES

Makes 6

'Don't eat the roses, Kiki!' I've said that a few times. We actually had to get rid of the roses in our garden because she kept eating them when she was little! I thought, how cool would it be if I could make a delicious rose lookalike treat for Kiki to enjoy? The apple rose was born. You've probably guessed by now that I love using puff pastry. It's an amazing base to get creative with, plus it lasts for months in the freezer. With a thaw time of just 10 minutes, you honestly can't go wrong. What I love about this dish is the simple, quick method and the super awesome result. Let's get to it!

1 sheet of frozen puff pastry, thawed

1 pink lady apple, cored, halved and finely sliced

1 tablespoon unsalted butter

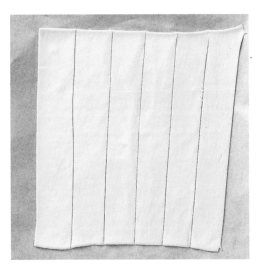

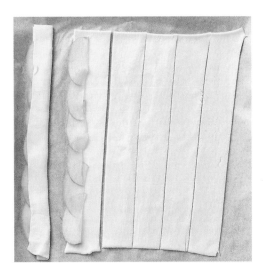

1. Preheat the oven to 180°C. Line a baking tray with baking paper. Cut the puff pastry into 5 cm-wide strips. Pop the apple and butter in a bowl and cook in the microwave on high for 40 seconds. The butter will melt and soften the apple.

2. Place the apple slices along the length of each pastry strip, with the rounded apple edges slightly hanging over the edge. Fold the pastry over the apple to secure it, but make sure the apple edges are still visible.

3. Now the rolling process begins. It's important to roll tightly, but to also make sure you don't lose any apple slices. Steady as she goes, roll up one pastry length into a coil. Give the end a slight squeeze to secure, then repeat with the remaining pastry lengths.

4. Transfer the apple roses to the prepared tray and bake for 20 minutes until golden and cooked through. The pastries can be eaten hot or cold. Serve in a school lunchbox or take them to work and be the envy of your colleagues.

 Try using pear slices instead of apple.
For a sweeter treat, sprinkle over a little cinnamon or even honey (as pictured).

STRAWBERRY 'POP TARTS'

Makes 4

When I was a kid, I remember watching a TV advertisement where Pop Tarts would fly out of the toaster. Everyone was smiling, while filling their bodies with a heap of additives and sugars. This recipe emulates the treat, but without the bad stuff. I figured they surely can't be hard to make, and guess what? They're not. So, I bought a punnet of strawberries and a loaf of bread, pulled out the toaster and bang, within minutes I'd made my own version of the Strawberry Pop Tart. I decided to call them ... Strawberry 'Pop Tarts'.

4 slices of wholemeal bread

1 cup hulled strawberries, sliced 0.5 cm thick

ground cinnamon, for sprinkling

1. Cut the crusts off the bread and freeze them for another use. Roll the bread nice and thin using a rolling pin.

2. Place the sliced strawberries on one half of each bread slice, leaving 1 cm of space around the edges.

3. Fold the bread over the strawberries and, using your fingers, pinch the edges to seal.

4. Crimp the edges with a fork, then pop your pop tarts in the toaster and toast to your liking. Sprinkle a little cinnamon on top and don't hold back. Delicious and simple.

 TIPS Feel free to use blueberries or other berries instead of strawberries. You can also make these 'pop tarts' in a frying pan with butter and cinnamon.

APPLE & BLUEBERRY BR-UFFINS

Makes 6

The number-one question I am asked on my social media pages is what to do with bread offcuts. Now, as much as I'd like to say I take my daughters to feed the ducks at the lake (I don't because we don't have a lake near us, plus bread is bad for ducks), I hate wasting food and I always try to be as resourceful as possible. Apart from shovelling bread down my throat when I'm making lunches, I now tend to pop the offcuts in a zip-lock bag in the freezer and save them to make these awesome apple and blueberry br-uffins.

4 cups roughly chopped bread offcuts, thawed if frozen

1 apple, cored and sliced

2 teaspoons ground cinnamon

butter, for greasing (optional)

handful of blueberries

1. Preheat the oven to 175°C. Drop the bread offcuts into a blender, then add the apple and cinnamon and blitz for 20–25 seconds until the ingredients are nice and evenly chopped.

2. Grease a six-hole muffin tin or line with paper cases. Spoon the mixture evenly into the holes and press it in lightly with the back of a spoon.

3. Grab the blueberries and pop them on top of the br-uffins, pushing them into the mixture, but leaving them half exposed.

4. Pop the tin in the oven for 10 minutes or until the br-uffins are golden brown. They're delicious eaten warm, but will also keep in an airtight container in the fridge for up to 3 days.

TIP If you don't have any blueberries, ½ cup of raisins or dates will also work a treat.

MYSTERY PUFFS

Makes 9

We've all heard the phrase 'don't play with your food'. Well … it's time to play with your food! In fact, it's a game the whole family can play. Using my favourite ingredient, puff pastry, you can make eating veggies and other foods kids often turn their noses up at into a lucky-dip game. So, let's make broccoli and cauliflower fun again by playing mystery puff roulette!

oil spray, for greasing

2 sheets of frozen puff pastry, thawed

2 broccoli florets

1 cauliflower floret

2 marshmallows

2 cherry or mini roma tomatoes

¼ carrot, diced

2 milk chocolate buttons

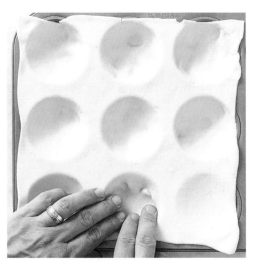

1. Preheat the oven to 180°C. Lightly grease nine holes of a muffin tin. Lay a pastry sheet on top of the muffin tin. Being careful not to tear the pastry, gently press it down into each hole until you can touch the base of the tin.

2. Now for the fun part. Fill each hole with a secret ingredient. Get your children to help put the fillings in.

3. Lay the second sheet of pastry over the top and cut into nine squares using a knife. Pop the tin in the oven for 15–17 minutes until golden brown.

4. Remove the puffs from the oven and allow them to cool slightly before tipping them into a large mixing bowl. It's lucky-dip time! The number-one rule of the game is that you have to eat what you pick in its entirety. Enjoy!

TIP As a grown-up, it's your responsibility to cheat, which means you might secretly mark the chocolate pastry so it is only identifiable to you. The idea is to lead by example, so you must also eat the mystery puff, even if it contains the cauliflower.

BR-ICHE

Makes 6

I love a quiche, but I always thought they were too fancy to make for lunchboxes; that is, until I dug out the protein shaker from the back of my cupboard. Instead of using a traditional pastry crust, I decided to make my own using dinner rolls. When I tried them, I realised just how perfect they were for lunchboxes. By combining dinner rolls and a quiche filling, the br-iche was born. I immediately ate the first six that I made without sharing a single one.

6 white or wholemeal dinner rolls

2 eggs

2 tablespoons melted butter

¾ cup milk (use lactose-free, soy or almond milk if you prefer)

½ cup grated mozzarella

½ cup diced ham off the bone

¼ cup diced capsicum (try a mix of red, green and yellow – they'll look even more awesome!)

⅓ cup self-raising flour

1. Preheat the oven to 180°C. Using a knife, cut the bread rolls open and get the kids to help pull the bread out of the middle, leaving just the crusty shells. Freeze the pulled-out bread in a zip-lock bag to use in another recipe (such as my br-uffins on page 172). Place the bread rolls on a baking tray.

2. Place the remaining ingredients in a protein shaker, adding the flour last. Pop the lid on, making sure it is firmly secured (cleaning the kitchen ceiling isn't fun!), and shake for about 1 minute until well combined.

3. Pour the mixture into the prepared bread rolls until they are three-quarters full.

4. Place in the oven and bake for 25 minutes or until golden brown on top. Store the br-iches in the fridge for up to 5 days or in the freezer for up to 3 months. Br-iches are perfect for school lunchboxes as they can be eaten cold. They also make a great dinner option for fussy little peeps.

 TIP **Experiment with different fillings and have fun with them. Leftover veggies are awesome, as is shredded chicken instead of ham.**

PIZZA SCROLL

Serves 1

Who doesn't love pizza? If you answered 'me' please email me, we need to talk. If you're a pizza lover, like everyone in my little family, you'll love this simple recipe. I have a few close friends, but my best friend is the frozen puff pastry you buy from the supermarket. It sits in the freezer waiting for me to turn it into many delicious recipes. Here I turn it into pizza scrolls, which are great for dinners and parties as well as lunchboxes. Try combining two or three puff pastry sheets to make one giant pizza scroll that you can share with a loved one (or not).

1 sheet of frozen puff pastry, thawed

2 tablespoons pizza sauce

½ cup grated mozzarella

1. Preheat the oven to 180°C and line a baking tray with baking paper. Grab a sharp knife and cut the puff pastry in half. Now make a long rectangle of pastry by overlapping the short end of one piece onto the end of the other and pressing to seal.

2. Spread the pizza sauce evenly over the pastry, leaving a 1–2 cm border around the edges. Sprinkle the grated mozzarella over the pizza sauce. If you're a cheese addict, just add more.

3. Using both hands, lift the pastry edge closest to you and roll up the pastry to look like a long sausage roll.

4. Starting at one end, coil the sausage and roll inwards to look like a large snail. Pop it on the prepared tray and into the oven for 20 minutes. You can also top the scroll with extra pizza sauce and cheese before putting it in the oven. Once cooked, enjoy it straight away or freeze for up to 3 months.

 TIP You can add any of your favourite pizza toppings, even pineapple if you're that way inclined. Does pineapple belong on pizza? Hmm.

VEGETABLE DOUGHNUTS

Makes 6

This creation of mine was, a huge hit with my little family – the word doughnut is enough to make any kid hyper. So, let me introduce my veggie doughnut. The good thing about this doughnut is that it uses colourful vegetables and zero sugar. I love the idea that you can tell your friends you're always using your protein shaker, but you don't have to tell them exactly what for. Serving doughnuts in school lunchboxes has never been so cool. If you don't have a doughnut muffin tin a regular muffin tin will work, but your doughnuts will look less doughnut-y.

¼ **cup vegetable oil, plus extra for greasing**

¾ **cup milk (use lactose-free, soy or almond milk if you prefer)**

1 egg

1 cup self-raising flour

¾ **cup grated cheddar**

½ **cup diced colourful vegetables (I used red, green and yellow capsicum here, but use any veggies or herbs that you like. My youngest, Kiki, loves tomato and basil.)**

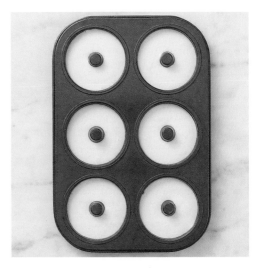

1. Preheat the oven to 180°C. Lightly grease six holes of a doughnut muffin tin. Unscrew the lid of your protein shaker and add the oil, milk and egg, followed by the self-raising flour. Close the lid tight and shake it until you feel your arm dislodging itself from its socket, or 1 minute; whichever comes first.

2. Open the lid and pour the mixture into the muffin tin holes until they are three-quarters full.

3. Sprinkle the cheese and diced veggies over the top of the doughnuts. The vegetables are meant to represent hundreds and thousands, so use a mixture of colours to make them look awesome.

4. Pop the tin in the oven for 20 minutes or until the doughnuts are cooked through. Leave to cool in the tin, then pop them straight into school lunchboxes or keep them in an airtight container in the fridge for up to 4 days or in the freezer for up to 3 months.

 TIP Vegetable doughnuts can be eaten warm from the oven, cold or even reheated in the microwave – just zap them for 15 seconds.

BR-USHI

Serves 2

How is it that one of my girls loves sushi and the other can't handle the sight of seaweed? I felt like my eldest was missing out, so I decided to come up with a solution. That solution is called br-ushi: a simple combination of bread rolls and sushi rolls. What I didn't realise when I created them was just how awesome they would look! I love serving them on a platter with avocado in a separate little bowl to look like wasabi. I almost felt like Heston with this one.

2 white or wholemeal dinner rolls

2 × 95 g cans tuna in spring water, drained (or use shredded chicken or rice)

2 teaspoons mayonnaise

2 carrots, cut into 5 cm long batons (or use celery)

2 baby cucumbers, quartered lengthways

1 avocado, mashed smooth to look like wasabi

soy sauce, for dipping

1. Place each roll on its end and, using a spoon handle, press the insides in to make a hollow in the roll, making as much room as possible for your filling.

2. Combine the tuna and mayonnaise in a small bowl and start filling the rolls. Keep packing it in: the idea is to stuff it nice and tight. You should be able to fit a whole can of tuna into each roll.

3. Now grab the carrot batons and push them in around the tuna, then do the same with the cucumber. You should feel the bread rolls getting firm and a little heavy; this means you're are ready to make some br-ushi!

4. Grab a chopping board and a sharp knife and cut each filled roll into 1.5 cm-wide slices, so they resemble sushi. How awesome do they look? Serve your br-ushi with the avocado 'wasabi' on the side and some soy sauce for dipping.

 TIP Br-ushi are great for platters at parties, as well as in school or work lunchboxes.

CHEESY CHICKEN NUGGETS

Makes 8–10

Nuggets. The word alone is enough to freak me out. I've tried every trick in the book to convince my girls that they're not healthy and, in fact, kind of evil. But dip them in sauce and kids go nuts for them, so I had to step in and create my own version of the cheesy chicken nugget.

1 cooked chicken breast, sliced (or use cooked lamb or beef)

½ cup grated cheddar

3 slices of wholemeal bread (or 3 cups roughly chopped bread offcuts)

oil spray, for greasing (optional)

2 tablespoons tomato sauce or barbecue sauce

1. Preheat the oven to 180°C or an air-fryer on medium heat. In a blender or food processor, blitz the chicken, cheese and bread for about 30 seconds until the ingredients are well combined.

2. Transfer to a bowl and shape tablespoons of the mixture into nuggets. You can even get fancy and use cookie cutters to create some awesome shapes.

3. If cooking the nuggets in the oven, pop them on a greased baking tray and bake for 10–12 minutes. Alternatively, drop them in the air-fryer for 5–6 minutes.

4. While the nuggets are cooking, divide the sauce among dipping bowls, then wait for the magic to come out of the oven. Once ready, let them cool down a little and yell out to the kids to get in the kitchen.

TIPS Getting the kids to shape their own nuggets means they're more likely to actually eat them. These are best eaten freshly baked, but are great in lunchboxes, too.

FILO PASTRY THINGY

Serves 1

When I was a little kid, many, many years ago, my mum used to spend hours in the kitchen making a traditional Macedonian dish called maznik. I remember it being delicious. When I recently asked my mum for the recipe, I almost fell over when I saw just how complicated it was. If I was going to make it, it had to be simplified, as there was no way I was going to make filo pastry from scratch. Thankfully, I found frozen filo pastry in the supermarket and so my new creation was born. If you are Macedonian and make this the traditional way, you best turn over the page now or your life might change forever.

1 sheet of frozen filo pastry

½ cup crumbled feta (or be adventurous and try different varieties of cheese – imagine blue cheese, pear and walnut?)

1 egg, beaten

1 teaspoon sesame seeds

cherry tomatoes, cucumber and plain yoghurt, to serve (optional)

1. Preheat the oven to 180°C or an air-fryer to medium. Gently lay the filo pastry on a clean bench with the long edge facing you. Spoon a good helping of feta along the middle third of the pastry sheet, leaving a 4 cm border at both ends. Don't be shy with the feta, you can load it up!

2. Now for the fun part: fold over the short edges to enclose the feta, then, starting with the long edge closest to you, roll up the pastry and feta into a long, tight roll.

3. Grab one end of the filo and feta roll and start coiling inwards to make a large snail shape. Brush the top with the beaten egg and sprinkle with sesame seeds.

4. If cooking the pastry thingy in the oven, place it on a baking tray lined with baking paper and bake for 15–18 minutes. Alternatively, pop it in the air-fryer for 7 minutes. Once cooked, it should be golden brown and looking mighty fine. Serve straight away or allow it to cool and pop it in a lunchbox.

 TIP As an alternative filling, try using ½ cup each of grated pumpkin and spinach. How awesome would that be?

CU-SHI ROLLS

Makes 5–6

California rolls are pretty awesome, but when one of my girls found out that they were held together by seaweed she thought I was joking. She realised I wasn't and hasn't touched another California roll since! I had to figure out a way to get her to enjoy the concept of sushi, especially because the ingredients are always so healthy. Cucumber was the first vegetable that came to mind as a replacement for the seaweed, so here is my cu-shi creation! Cu-shi rolls make awesome party food – they look super cool on a platter.

1 large cucumber

1 × 95 g tin tuna in spring water, drained

1 tablespoon mayonnaise

1 carrot, cut into matchsticks

soy sauce and wasabi, to serve (optional)

1. Peel long ribbons of cucumber and place them on a paper towel to remove excess moisture. Keep going until you've peeled the whole cucumber, avoiding the central seeds if you can as they tend to be a little bitter.

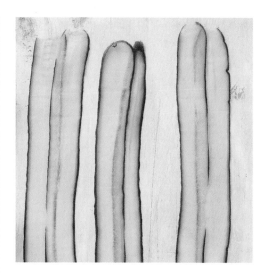

2. Overlap two cucumber strips by about 1 cm. This will be your seaweed replacement.

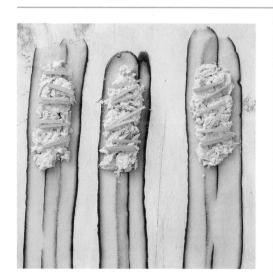

3. Combine the tuna and mayonnaise in a small bowl. Spoon a little of the tuna mixture onto the cucumber strips, followed by a few carrot matchsticks.

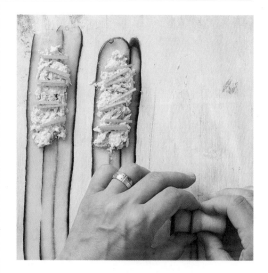

4. Roll up the cucumber strips nice and tight. Some ingredients may fall out the sides, but that's totally cool – consider them your reward. Use a sharp knife to neaten the edges, then repeat with the remaining ingredients to make 5–6 cu-shi rolls. Pop them into lunchboxes in a cooler bag with an ice pack, and send the kids off to school.

 TIP Other awesome fillings include rice, chicken and other vegetables, such as celery, capsicum or broccoli.

AUSSIE TACO PIES

Makes 6

One day, while waiting to buy a meat pie at the local footy food van,
I noticed the owner of the van was standing outside on a break. He was
wearing a Mexican-themed T-shirt, so I asked him why didn't he sell Mexican
food instead of meat pies? He said it wasn't practical for the footy because
Mexican food can be messy. Then I had a light-bulb moment: why not combine
the meat pie with a Tex-Mex taco? At that moment my Aussie taco pies were
born. It's amazing how the simplest of things can inspire us.

2 sheets of frozen puff pastry, thawed

oil spray, for greasing

250 g beef mince (or use chicken mince)

1 × 30 g packet taco spice mix

1 cup grated cheddar

sour cream or plain yoghurt, to serve

1 avocado, roughly mashed

1. Preheat the oven to 180°C. Using a cookie cutter or your favourite coffee cup, cut out 12 circles from the puff pastry. Grab a muffin tin and lightly grease the holes with oil spray. Line the holes with half the puff pastry circles.

2. Heat a frying pan over medium heat and add the mince. Sprinkle over the spice mix and cook for 6–8 minutes. You don't need to cook the mince all the way through as it will finish cooking in the oven. Remove from the heat and set aside to cool.

3. Fill the pastry cases with the mince mixture until they are three-quarters full. Sprinkle over the cheese and place the remaining puff pastry circles on top.

4. Gently squeeze the pastry edges to seal, then pop in the oven and bake for 15–20 minutes until golden brown. Dollop some sour cream or plain yoghurt on top of the pies and finish with a spoon of mashed avocado or use it as a dip. Enjoy, amigos.

 TIP Pop any leftover pies in the fridge once completely cold and pack them in school lunchboxes the next day – way cool.

CHEESE & SALAMI SCROLLS

Makes 3

Cheese and salami sandwiches are a bit of a lunchbox staple, I reckon.
Now that I'm in charge of school lunches, I try and mix it up for my girls,
so I wanted to make a cheese and salami creation that was a little more
exciting than plain old sandwiches. I soon figured out a way to bake
the ingredients, which not only made them look super, but also fit perfectly
into lunchboxes.

**6 slices of wholemeal bread, crusts cut off
and frozen in a zip-lock bag for another
use (see page 21)**

3 slices of cheddar

9 thin slices of mild salami

1. Preheat the oven to 180°C or an air-fryer to medium. Overlap two bread slices by about 2 cm, then repeat with the remaining bread slices. Grab a rolling pin or wine bottle and roll the overlapping bread nice and thin to help the slices stick together. Trim the edges so they look neat.

2. Lay out the bread with the shortest end facing you. Cut each slice of cheese into three lengths and lay the cheese along one long side of the joined bread slices. Top with the salami slices, so they slightly hang over the edge.

3. Fold the bread over to enclose the filling and gently press the bread so nothing falls out (kind of like putting the kids to bed). Now roll up the bread into three scrolls. Add toothpicks to secure if needed.

4. If cooking the scrolls in the oven, place them on a baking tray lined with baking paper and bake for 10 minutes. Alternatively, pop them in the air-fryer for 5 minutes. They look awesome, are fun to eat and make a great after-school snack, too.

 TIPS **Feel free to use ham instead of salami.**
If you want to get fancy you can even butter the bread on the outside before placing it in the oven or air-fryer.

BR-YOZA

Makes 5

How delicious are traditional Japanese gyoza? What I love most about them is how you can hide herbs inside to make them even more healthy for the kids. However, there is no way I can make the wrappers; I ain't got time for that. So, I decided to create my very own 'dad' version that's easy, delicious and just the right size for a bite-sized snack. Step forward the br-yoza. (I think I've single-handedly destroyed the English and Japanese languages with this recipe title!)

5 slices of wholemeal bread

1 cup finely sliced or shredded leftover chicken (or use a freshly cooked chicken breast or any other cooked meat of your choice)

½ cup grated cheddar

large handful of finely chopped herbs and/or vegetables (optional)

1 tablespoon olive oil or butter

soy sauce or sweet chilli sauce, for dipping (optional)

1. Using a cookie cutter or an upturned cup, cut circles out of the bread slices. Don't throw away the leftover bread – freeze it to use in one of my other creations (see page 21). Grab a rolling pin or your favourite wine bottle and roll out the bread slices until they're nice and thin.

2. Place a bread circle in your hand and slightly cup it with your palm. Add one-fifth of the chicken followed by one-fifth of the grated cheese. (Remember this is the part where you can also hide finely chopped herbs and veggies inside; just don't get busted by your little humans!)

3. Using your other hand, fold over the bread circle to enclose the filling and pinch the edges together nice and tight. You've just made your first br-yoza! Repeat with the remaining bread and filling.

4. Fire up the frying pan over medium heat and add the oil or butter. Drop in your br-yozas and let them toast up until they are golden brown. Flip them over and toast the other side. Remove from the pan and let them cool for lunchboxes or serve them up nice and hot, with soy or sweet chilli sauce for dipping.

 TIPS Br-yoza will keep in an airtight container in the fridge for 2–3 days. They can be eaten cold or reheated in the microwave for 8 seconds to warm them up.

Place them on a bed of noodles or rice to take them up a notch!

DAFFODILS

Makes 6

The daffodil is such a happy flower. It's bright, yellow and, to me, represents sunshine. So why not recreate them using food for our children to enjoy? Who would have thought that by using simple ingredients we could recreate happiness? I wonder if I made a few of these for my better half on Valentine's Day I could avoid buying her flowers ... I'll keep you posted.

oil spray, for greasing
6 wholemeal wraps
1 cup grated cheese
6 eggs
salt and pepper (optional)

1. Preheat the oven to 160°C. Lightly grease six holes of a muffin tin. Using a knife or a pizza cutter, cut two semicircles from each wrap. We don't actually need the leftover rectangles, but don't throw them out as they're great for making spring-wiches (see page 209).

2. Pop a semicircle of wrap in one of the holes so the two corners are pointing upwards. Place another semicircle crossways over the first wrap, also with the corners pointing upwards. Repeat with the remaining wrap semicircles.

3. Sprinkle the cheese into the wraps and crack the eggs on top of the cheese. Season with salt and pepper, if you like.

4. Pop the muffin tin in the oven and bake for 15 minutes or until the egg is cooked through. Keep an eye on the edges of the wraps as they can easily burn. The daffodils look amazing on a platter and my girls love them in their lunchboxes.

 TIPS Kiki, my youngest, loves her eggs runny so she can snap off the wrap edges and dip them into the yolk. She's a clever little one.

You can use different-flavoured wraps, such as garlic and herb, which adds an extra-delicious flavour.

SPILL-PROOF KEBABS

Makes 6

Every time I think of a kebab it reminds me of being driven home in a taxi late at night while slightly intoxicated, wishing the driver would stop at one those kebab stands on the side of the road. Just for the record, this doesn't happen often, maybe only three or four times a week (just kidding!).

The worst part of the whole kebab experience is the drippage, droppage and loss of delicious ingredients. Something needed to be done, so here's introducing my spill-proof kebabs designed for little humans. The best time to make these is the day after you make lamb cutlets or chicken for dinner, so make sure you cook extra and have leftovers.

3 wholemeal pita pockets

**leftover cooked lamb or chicken
(around 90 g), sliced**

4 tomatoes, chopped

1 cup plain yoghurt

handful of spinach leaves

1. Using a knife or a pizza cutter, cut a strip out of the middle of each pita pocket to make two semicircles per pocket. We don't actually need the leftover strips, but don't throw them away as you can use them to make some of my other creations (see page 21 for ideas).

2. Open up the pita pocket semicircles so they look like little boats.

3. Fill each pita boat with the lamb or chicken, tomato and yoghurt, then top with the spinach.

4. Because the meat is already cold, it's fine to make these the night before, refrigerate and pop them into school lunchboxes in the morning.

TIPS Be brave and add a few slices of red onion; it works so well in kebabs.
Put these on a platter when guests come over and impress your friends.
Try using tzatziki instead of plain yoghurt for a garlic hit.

PARTY PASTIES

Makes 12

I love pasties, especially pasties that have crispy pastry and a dollop of sauce to cool down the hot ingredients. However, I often find that they're too big for little ones, so, me being me, I decided to children-ise (before you look that up, I'll tell you now that it's not a real word, but it means making something for children that's generally for adults) my own version of the pastie. There are party pies and party sausage rolls, but I've never found any party pasties. So here they are!

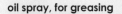

oil spray, for greasing

3 sheets of frozen puff pastry, thawed

1 porterhouse steak (about 200 g), roughly chopped

1 potato, roughly chopped

2 carrots, roughly chopped

salt and pepper

1 × 125 g can sweet corn kernels, drained

1 cup frozen peas

tomato sauce, to serve

1. Preheat the oven to 180°C. Lightly grease a baking tray with oil spray. Using an upside-down mug, cut out circles of puff pastry. If you don't have an upside-down mug, just use a normal mug and turn it upside down.

2. Place the steak, potato and carrot in a blender. Blitz until the mixture looks like a mash of red veggies, then transfer to a bowl. Season with salt and pepper and stir through the corn and peas.

3. Using a tablespoon, dollop the mixture in the centre of the puff pastry circles.

4. Fold over the pastry circles, then crimp the edges with a fork or your fingers to tightly seal. Pop the pasties on the prepared tray and bake for 20–25 minutes until golden. Serve with tomato sauce on the side.

TIPS
You can make the party pasties any size you like.
Try adding different veggies to the mixture.
This is a great recipe to hide extra veg in.

TACO TUGBOATS

Makes 8

Pita pockets are an awesome alternative to sliced bread, and the fact that you can get wholemeal varieties makes them even healthier. While playing in the kitchen recently, I figured out how to turn simple pita pockets into cool little boats (or tugboats as my daughter Anela calls them). By filling them with fresh and delicious ingredients, I created an irresistible taco-inspired lunchbox treat for my girls. But the best thing about this simple creation is that you can fill them with any ingredients you like. You can make them sweet or savoury and enjoy them for breakfast, lunch or dinner – they're awesome for kids' parties, too.

4 wholemeal pita pockets

4 mini cucumbers, diced

1 × 125 g can sweet corn kernels, drained

3 tomatoes, diced

½ cup mild salsa

1 cup grated cheddar

½ cup sour cream (or plain yoghurt)

1. Preheat the oven to 180°C. Using a knife or a pizza cutter, cut a strip out of the middle of each pita pocket to make two semicircles per pocket.

2. Now push the bottoms of the pita pocket semicircles as if you were turning a sock inside-out, but don't turn the whole way; just enough for them to look like little boats. Did it work? Good, continue.

3. Cut triangles out of the leftover pita strips. The idea is to make them look like nacho chips. Get it? Awesome. Pop the tugboats and pita triangles in the oven for 10 minutes to crisp up a little, just like nacho chips.

4. Fill the tugboats with the cucumber, sweet corn and tomato, then top with some salsa, grated cheese and a dollop of sour cream. Pop the pita triangles on top so they look like little flags for the boats. Place them in school lunchboxes or on a platter if you're eating them straight away.

 TIP **Create as many tugboats as you like and fill them with different ingredients. Try making a dessert tugboat by filling it with sliced banana, yoghurt and berries.**

MAKING SANDWICHES FUN AGAIN

One of my biggest challenges has been to figure out how to get my girls to enjoy wholegrain bread. Sandwiches are boring, and I often remember tossing mine in the bin as soon as the home-time bell rang. My sister and I perfected the art of throwing out our sandwiches. Sorry Mum.

One day, while eating at our favourite Thai restaurant, I was watching my girls devour their food. If only I could make dumplings and spring rolls out of bread. A brainwave hit me and there was no time for dessert; I had to race home and try my new ideas. They worked! We named the spring roll sandwich the spring-wich, the dumpling sandwich the sand-ling and the ravioli sandwich the rav-wich.

Use the below ingredients to make as many of the following creations as you like and see page 21 for ideas for all of the bread offcuts.

wholemeal bread slices

deli ham slices off the bone

grated cheese

SPRING-WICH

1. Remove the crusts from a bread slice and use a rolling pin to flatten the bread.

2. Place a slice of ham on the bottom half of the bread and sprinkle some cheese on top.

3. Fold in the left and right sides by 1 cm and then, starting from the bottom, roll up the bread into a spring roll, or spring-wich.

4. Repeat with more bread, ham and cheese to make as many spring-wiches as you like.

RAV-WICH

1. Remove the crusts from two bread slices and use a rolling pin to flatten the bread.

2. Place a small amount of ham and cheese in the four corners of one bread slice.

3. Lay the other bread slice on top and use a ravioli or pasta cutter to cut it into four squares.

4. You've just made four rav-wiches! Now repeat with more bread, ham and cheese.

SAND-LING

1. Use an upside-down mug to cut out a round of bread from one bread slice.

2. Place the bread in your palm and start clapping a few times to lightly flatten the bread.

3. While still holding the bread in your palm, place some ham and a sprinkle of cheese in the centre of the bread.

4. Fold over the bread and pinch the edges tightly to seal the ingredients.

TIPS You can use any combination of fillings in these creations. Let your imagination run wild!
All of the above taste awesome pan-fried with a little butter.
I also love popping these creations on a bed of carrot noodles, which makes them look super cool.

THANKS

Carrie Felton and the Stuck On You crew without your guidance and advice none of this would have been possible.

Warren Freeman love you, bro. You're my angel and dearest friend. Cupine!

Mary Small is this happening? The best publisher on the planet, thank you for believing in me.

Jane Winning and Clare Marshall you guys rock. Thank you.

Ash Carr you're awesome, we need more beans. I'm stoked my book was your first project.

Georgia Gold you're the way awesome photographer with a heart of gold.

Karina Duncan your styling is amazing, you're a huge talent with an awesome soul.

Emma Roocke chef extraordinaire, thank you for rocking my recipes.

Kirby Armstrong thank you for your incredible designs and for bringing my vision to reality.

Lucy Heaver editor extraordinaire, thanks for all your hard work.

Julia Ferracane you believed in me from the beginning and your amazing work got me to where I am. Thank you times infinity.

Gayle Oznobyshyn-Hicks from day one you saw this coming, thank you for pushing and making it happen. I appreciate everything you've done for me.

Eddie Vedder from Pearl Jam we still have time to be together.

Dad no words will ever do my feelings justice. You are so missed, and after 22 years I still feel the pain of not having you here.

My mum *insert crying* I'm too emotional to write just how I feel. I know that you know how much I love you, for the strength you've shown since Dad passed away. You inspire me to be me.

My darling sister, Suzy no words can describe our connection and till our last breath you will always be my big sister. I love you.

Vince, my bro love you for everything you've done for me.

Lachlan and Julian please outgrow your Nikes so you can give them to your uncle. Love you both very much.

To each and every one of my followers on Instagram and Facebook please high five yourselves. You have all brought out the best in me. Thank you so much.

And of course, thank you to my darling wife, Marina, and to my girls, Anela and Kiara.

INDEX

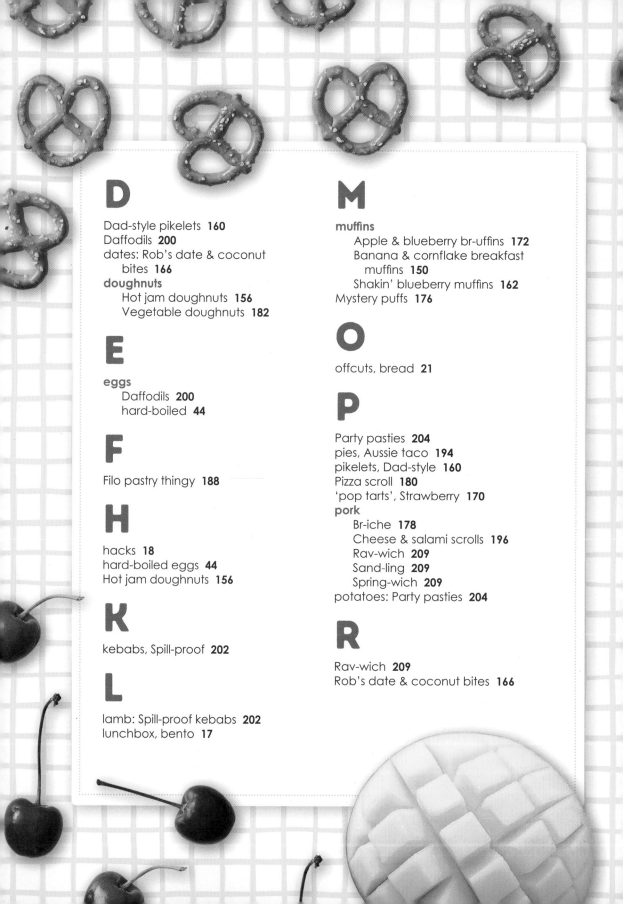

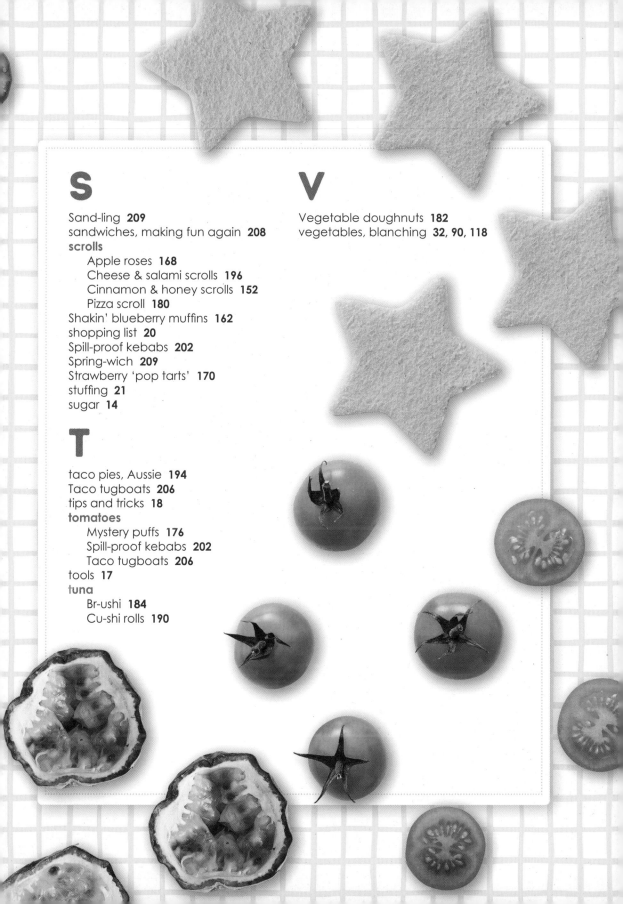

A Plum book
First published in 2019 by
Pan Macmillan Australia Pty Limited
Level 25, 1 Market Street,
Sydney, NSW 2000, Australia

Level 3, 112 Wellington Parade,
East Melbourne, VIC 3002, Australia

Design by Kirby Armstrong
Edited by Lucy Heaver
Index by Helena Holmgren
Photography by Georgia Gold
Prop and food styling by Karina Duncan
Food preparation by George Georgievski and Emma Roocke
Typeset by Post Pre-press Group
Colour reproduction by Splitting Image Colour Studio
Printed and bound in China by 1010 Printing International Limited

A CIP catalogue record for this book is available from the National Library
of Australia.

The publisher would like to thank Stuck On You for their generosity
in providing props for the book.

10 9 8 7 6 5 4 3 2 1